A PARENT GUIDE:

Helping Your Children Raise You!

(MY STORIES)

Don Peterson

ISBN: 0692261605

ISBN 13: 9780692261606

Acknowledgement

Thanks Tracey!!!!

Table of Contents

Introduction

Ready or Not, Here He Comes

Tracey, my wife, laid in the bathtub with hot water covering the enlarged belly that contained our second child. She had a look of peace on her face even though she had just completed another contraction. I was kneeling next to the tub. Checking for the baby, I felt his head crown. Panic ran through my body; my pulse increased. I gave my wife a fake, reassuring smile and said, "The baby is coming."

She replied, with a voice meant to calm me, "I know."

I literally ran out of the bathroom, knowing I had little time before the next contraction. Now that Tracey could not see me, I allowed the fear to surface. The first thing I did was call the midwife (yes, we were having a home birth). She informed me that her car had broken down and she was not going to make it. Next, I ran to the front door, looked up and down the street for anyone who might be out at three o'clock in the morning, and said in a panicked voice to myself, "God, I will take anyone to help. Let someone be there." No one was outside; God was merciful to my neighbors.

Finally, against my wife's wishes, I called 911 and told them we were about to have a baby. I took a deep breath, put that fake smile back on my face, and went back into the bathroom.

I breathed through the next couple of contractions with Tracey, and I realized the baby was coming *now*. Despite her being very comfortable with having the baby under water, I was not, so I insisted that she get out of the tub.

She said, "OK, but you will need to help me."

I got behind her, put my arms under her arms, and pulled her over the tub wall. As her second leg cleared the wall, with me still behind her, she went into a squatting position, and our son Joey literally slid out onto the floor. While few people believe us, my wife's first words after the birth were, "That was easy." She continued to squat on the floor, picked up her baby, and began to nurse Joey. She glowed and smiled, and I could see the presence of God on her face. (By the way, the paramedics arrived after the baby came. My wife graciously let them check the baby, and then we sent them on their way.)

$$* \quad * \quad *$$

It took years to admit that my fear and panic existed because I was not receptive to God's grace. I was very committed to my opinion that childbirth was scary. Conversely, my wife's peace and tranquility in the midst of birth was only possible because she was living in His grace. This is one of our early experiences of letting our child rearing (in this case, birthing) develop our awareness of how God's grace works and transcends all fleshly thinking.

This book is designed to emphasize the importance of contemplation, so you can be open to receiving God's grace and seeing how it works in your life. It is not meant to be a "Raising Your Children for Dummies" instruction guide. For this reason, the chapter titles are in the form of questions, so you will always be reminded that the questions are more important than the answers.

The chapters begin with a focusing concept, or principle, for you to think about, and at the end of the chapter, I give you questions to consider about how you might think about the principle presented in the chapter. Between the principle and questions, I will share family stories (either about my six children or the 120 people who have lived with us over the years) that will vividly describe where I or others fell short and how grace was made available to give me or others the eyes to see and ears to hear the principles to adopt. I trust you will find the stories entertaining; but please remember when reading them to look to see how God has used my children and others to help me be more like Christ.

It is considered normal, customary, and predictable that your children rebel against you when their hormones start raging. Many parents feel hopelessly out of touch with the young people in their houses. Yet God has a different plan, a different goal, and a remarkable context within which to raise your children. He does not desire you to be out of touch with them; He wants you to be one with them, as He is one with Christ

I am inviting you to consider that by reading this book, you will have the opportunity to alter your perspective on your parental role and to discover that your job may be "Helping Your Children Raise You." What if your children are the building blocks God uses to build your faith as you try to build their faith? Is it possible that your desire for a closer relationship with your children is the same desire we all have to move toward a closer relationship with Christ? Altering how you raise your children could be the key to more fully knowing Christ. While your children may benefit from you adopting some of the principles the book attempts to illuminate, the primary benefit that I hope for you is what Christ prayed for us all: that we become one as He and the Father are one (John 10:30).

I originally started writing this book as a way to pass the principles I have learned down to my children and their children. The best way I could think to pass on these principles was to capture some of our family stories and pass down my struggles and my victories through the telling of them. I hope these stories stimulate your thinking and pique your curiosity about how your relationship with your children is a mirror of your relationship with your Heavenly Father.

Proverbs 10:19 says, "In many words there is much transgression." I have written over twenty thousand words, so obviously I will be wrong about some things. Therefore, I encourage you to consider the concepts and principles and whether you want to embrace them, reject them, modify them, dwell on them, or ignore them. If you are willing to consider which principles will work for your family, even if you ultimately reject them, the purpose of my book will have been accomplished: you will be considering what principles will work for your family.

While similar principles and concepts have been taught and written about by many other men, more scholarly and holy than me, God uses many different methods to communicate to us. Maybe my storytelling is the method that will speak to your heart.

May God richly bless all the relationships in your home.

1

Who's Raising Whom?

Principle: Raising your children is a process that helps you to grow to be more like Christ by revealing the true condition of your heart.

I am a father of six children. At the time I started writing this book, my children ranged from three to eighteen years old; the youngest is now sixteen. I have three boys and three girls. The boys came first, and the girls came second. During my thirty-plus years of marriage to Tracey, we have had 120 different people live in our home. Some were friends we were helping; some were single mothers we were ministering to; some were children we were helping others raise; and, of course, we hosted other family members who needed a helping hand. We have had some remarkable success and some resounding failures over the years. The thing that is most clear to both Tracey and me is that our six children and 120 houseguests have all been used to "raise us" to be more like Christ.

Our most basic understanding is that while we are on this planet, we are to glorify God and our Lord Jesus. Without delving into a lengthy discussion or debate about what that means, suffice it to say that the Apostle Paul's synopsis would include running the race to win the prize by the renewing of our minds. Raising our children is not a distraction from winning the race but part of the fulfillment of it. Every circumstance will call for a response, and we will have automatic responses. Our automatic responses are indicators of the condition of our hearts. I am not sure that God uses circumstances to mold us, but I am sure that God uses circumstances to allow us to see our hearts and the condition of them. Seeing this perspective gives us the opportunity to make a real choice to alter our hearts. The current condition of one's heart is a result of current thinking about circumstances. By examining these stories, you might be challenged to change how you think about your current circumstances and to create a transformation of your heart.

The two stories below are examples of how God uses circumstances to reveal the condition of people's hearts through their responses. The first one is a tale of a young lady who seeks men to fill a hole in her heart, and the second is the tale of a father with anger in his heart.

STORY 1:
Rhonda Has a Date: Revelations of a Needy Heart

A number of years ago, a single, small fireball of a lady, who was about thirty years old (let's call her Rhonda) and her six-month-old child (let's call him Johnnie) lived with us because they had nowhere else to go. After Rhonda had been living with us for about six months, she brought a young man home for me to meet before she went on a date with him. We lived a little bit in the country, so to be polite, I walked out to his car, smiled, and stuck out my hand in the normal protective-father-type manner. He gave me a "chilling" grin and shook my hand. I instantly saw red lights and heard sirens (no, the police had not come yet). I asked Rhonda to come into the house and let me talk to her before she left. I begged and pleaded with her not to go with this man; I could not give valid reasons why, but I heard the soft voice of my heart telling me something was wrong. Well, she did not heed my warning and went off with him.

Later that evening Rhonda pulled up in her sedan and got little Johnnie out of the car. She was crying hysterically. It turns out that while

Rhonda was at someone's house, her date had become angry at his own son—who was about four years old—picked him up, and threw him down hard enough to cause a seizure. An ambulance was called, and the man said, "Rhonda, come with me to the hospital. I need you."

When the ambulance arrived, Rhonda, in a "reactive" mode, handed her baby to a stranger in the crowd that had formed around the ambulance. Rhonda did not know the person she handed her baby to, but she got into the ambulance with this man she had just met without her son. After the man's son was released from the hospital, Rhonda went back to find her baby and came home.

After hearing this story, I knew instantly why Rhonda was crying: God had revealed to her that her heart was predisposed to be given to a man at any cost; even the cost of her baby. It was a devastating insight for Rhonda to realize that her heart was so needy for a man's affection and approval that she had left her baby behind.

However, as I stood there in the driveway, helping her unload her trunk, I was smiling—not because I was right about the man but because God was speaking to my friend. I immediately told Rhonda, "We should stop now and pray right out here by the car and thank the Lord that He is still speaking to you. The Lord and God, who created the universe, is speaking to you about your heart. It is time to thank and praise Him." Rhonda and I prayed there in the driveway, and this was one of the turning points in her life. She started to learn how to transform her mind in a way that healed her heart. How can the heart truly heal without hearing the voice of its beloved Creator?

Here is what I want you to pull out of the story: Notice that the parental mistake she made with her baby provided an immediate insight into this man's heart, insight into her own heart, and finally insight into my heart. If I had chosen to react with an automatic response (such as, "I told you not to go with him! Do you know what you just did? You're not fit to be a mom!"), this scenario would likely not have had the same impact on Rhonda's heart. However, I was given the grace not to condemn and to make wrong, but to see where God was working so we could give thanks. If I had responded angrily or with arrogance, she would have had valid reasons to be upset with me. By responding with grace, I did not give her the opportunity to deflect the upset toward me. Instead, she saw that God was with her, providing for her, and speaking to her. It became a positive event rather than a devastating one because we focused on what God was doing rather than on her weaknesses or faults.

As parents, this is one obvious area for us to transform our thinking. When our children are disobedient, can we rejoice because we can see what God is doing and revealing? Can we help our children to see that God is still speaking to them? We aren't rejoicing because of sin, but we are rejoicing because God is still in our children's lives, and He is allowing them to see the condition of their hearts while revealing the condition of ours.

STORY 2:
The Evils of an Untucked Shirt:
Reversing Direction to Overcome Anger

All of my sons, including my eldest, were very well behaved and had excellent reputations in the church and in our community; however, even the best of boys makes mistakes from time to time.

My eldest son played basketball for a rather strict and very competitive homeschool team. This basketball team had very stringent rules, including the requirement that all players keep their shirts tucked in whenever they were with the team.

Well, during one tournament, a group of about four boys, including my son, decided to test the rules and showed up without their shirts tucked in (they were four of the starters for the team, of course). The coach saw them, and the next week, my son and I were called before the board, and he was suspended for a week. He was very upset about this.

On the outside, I talked a good game of how we had "agreed to the rules" and had to "respect authority." On the inside, I will admit I was having a good laugh about this. Imagine going to your Sunday school class where people are having problems with their kids having sex, drinking, or using drugs, and you share that your boy got suspended for not tucking in his shirt. It was rather humorous. However, I did not let on that I thought it was funny; I treated it as a serious matter, fully supporting the team and the rules. We abided by the suspension and made our apologies.

Later that week, we went to watch one of the games, and when my son walked out of the gym, he defiantly ripped his shirt out from his pants. Well, as we walked through the parking lot, I went ballistic, yelling at him, "This is exactly why you got suspended. You do not appreciate the effort I put in driving you around. You're supposed to be a Christian..." The longer I went, the louder I yelled and the redder my face became. (Now when this happens, my kids wonder if I am going to have a heart attack; I am getting up there in years.) My son did not reply. We drove along; I fumed, and he pretended to sleep and made it so that he did not have to talk to me by slouching in his seat and laying his head against the window.

Then I remembered this principle: circumstances are mirrors to be used to see the condition of the heart. It was very sobering to realize my heart held that much anger toward my son. It was scary to think that I might lose my relationship with my son if I could not transform my mind so my heart could release its anger. I quickly started thinking about how I could love my son in this circumstance to teach him and show mercy.

Being committed to creative solutions (see chapter 3), I thought, "Rather than yelling about how he dresses, I could show him how to dress."

This got me thinking: according to the basketball team's rules, not only were players' shirts to be tucked in but the players were not supposed to wear baggy pants that hung down low (the prevailing style) or do anything that drew undue attention to themselves—no funny hairstyles, no tattoos, no body piercing, and so on. The idea was for the players to dress and appear as men.

So as I sped down the freeway, two words came to my mind: Men's Wearhouse (a men's apparel shop). I decided to take him to the Men's Wearhouse and buy him some men's clothing. Arriving at the shop, I pulled into the parking lot and came to an abrupt stop (to wake him). He was a little groggy, and when he asked what we were doing, I said, "I am going to buy you the clothes you need to dress like a man."

We got out of the car. He walked about two steps behind me. When I opened the shop door, a very tall man (taller than my six-foot son) greeted me and asked what he could do for us. I stepped aside, put my arm around my son, and said, "You've got a $XX budget—teach this young man how to dress." (More about apologizing to your wife for overspending later.)

Well, this man was a gift from God. He called two other salespeople over, and they brought shirts, pants, sport coats, and ties for my son to choose from. They treated him as a very highly valued customer; it was beautiful. By now, my son was fighting to stay mad, but a little softness had started to appear in his expression. While this was going on, I said nothing. I stood to the side, just watching God work through this salesman to train my son.

After an hour or so, my son had picked out the clothes he wanted, and it was time for a fitting. So he went into the changing room, put on the new clothes, and then came out and stood in front of the mirrors. The salesman who'd greeted me at the door decided to do the fittings personally. So, this giant of a man knelt down before my son. He held his hands open, reached out, and put his hands on my son's waist. Looking up at him, he said, "This is a where a man wears his pants." Then he lowered his hands six inches, looked up at him again, and said, "This is where a boy wears his pants. Where would you like me to fit these pants you are buying?" Remember, I had not said a word, so this was a total shock to my son; he just stared down at the man in silence. The man did it again: he raised his hands, gripped my son's waist, and said, "This is where a man wears his pants." Again he lowered his hands and gripped below his hips on his legs and said, "This is where a boy wears his pants. For you, it seems like I should fit them somewhere in the middle." That is what the man did for my seventeen-year-old son.

We finished all the buying and drove home in silence. I believe God used the silence to have my son feel my love and to reveal to him the condition of my new heart. To this day, both he and I fondly remember that shopping trip as an experience we both learned from.

We can quickly identify sin in our hearts through the circumstances we find ourselves in and correct our actions in the middle of a circumstance. If I had recognized my anger but done nothing to show my love, this could have been a circumstance that created distance between my son and me. The midcourse correction turned this circumstance into a victory and an exciting story, rather than something my son could point to as just another time where Dad lost his temper.

My act of love robbed my son's heart of its ability to be angry. Though he tried to hang on to his anger, my act of love forced the anger out.

None of this would have been possible if I had not reflected upon the circumstances and asked myself what they revealed about my heart. I could have complained about the overly strict coaches, blamed the other kids he was with, or continued to stay mad at my son for his rebellion; instead, I was granted the grace to see my own sin and respond to my son's rebellion with love. All this came from asking the question "What is God showing me about the condition of my heart?"

SOMETHING TO CONSIDER

What have your actions today revealed about the condition of your heart?

Do you choose to keep the condition or change it?

2

Are You Living Your Life "Out of Context"?

Principle: God has a context within which to live your life: love.

Many of us have heard the phrase "You're taking the scripture out of context" when someone has quoted a Bible verse without recognition of the larger meaning of the passage or the circumstances in which the verse was written. Here I use "context" to mean the set of assumptions and beliefs that frame the events and circumstances of our lives. All of us, from time to time, live our lives "out of context." What do I mean? There are many contexts we can and do live from; but let me just give you two examples to consider.

CONTEXT 1:
Context Created from "Self"
Many of us live from the context that all of life's burdens and all of our parental mistakes make the situation dire. From this perspective, our mistakes can be seen as evidence of our lack of skill or fortitude or holiness or effort. We will forever reap the consequences of our mistakes, and so will our children—we can see it happening before our eyes. This sense

of urgency is compounded when we do give our best effort, and our children continue to make unhealthy choices and mistakes. We are left with a sense of resignation about changing the future, which can lead to either depression or withdrawal, along with a loss of affinity in the relationship.

At some point during the years of raising our children, many parents become discouraged, depressed, or resigned. Raising children forces us to make daily decisions about what to feed them, when to discipline, when to have mercy, when to be strict, when to grant freedoms, how many chores to give, where they should go to school, what classes they should take, what friends we should let them see, what friends we should forbid them to see, and so on. If we accept as truth that "All have sinned and fallen short of the glory of God" (Romans 3:23), then we know that we all make many mistakes over the years, and as the mistakes build and our children start making choices we do not like, discouragement and depression greet us when we get up in the morning.

CONTEXT 2:
God's Context

The universe itself exists in the context that God created. I am going to overly simplify it: the universe is designed to reveal Love and for us to express Love. If we raise our children consistent with this context, all of the burdens of life—the mistakes we make and the mistakes we are going to make—are opportunities to reveal and express love, and to train our children to love.

It is at this point that I encourage you to consider from what context you are living your life: Self-Context or God's Context.

Let me take a chance here, and I hope you will not judge me for being a little sacrilegious. Looking from a certain perspective, you could say the Father God failed when his son Adam and daughter Eve chose the wrong path and bit into the forbidden fruit. If God was living through our self-context (Context 1), the conversation between Him and Jesus might have gone like this (see John 1:1 and 1:12 to know Jesus was there with God when Adam was created):

Father and Jesus Discussion from Context 1: "Self" Context

Father: Did you see what Eve did? She talked Adam into disobeying.

Jesus: Yeah, we really blew it, didn't we? Where did we go wrong?

Father: Yeah, I knew I should have taken longer in making Adam. Doing it in one day just did not prepare him enough.

Jesus: Yeah, we could have given him more training before we gave in to his need for Eve. We should have prepared him more for the complications of a wife.

Father: We gave Adam authority over the whole garden! Boy, we should not have given him his freedom so soon. If only I had held on to the reins a little tighter, he would not have bitten into that fruit.

Jesus: Well, at least we could have planted the tree a little farther from their house; we simply were not protective enough of them. We blew that decision; if we had taken longer than a day making the earth, we could have designed the whole thing in a way that protected Adam and Eve from themselves.

Father: Speaking of protecting, what a mistake for us to think they could resist the serpent. I should have expelled him from the garden long before I made Eve. Only a totally miserable parent would be so negligent. I really was stupid about that decision.

Jesus: What is worse is that we saw it coming, and we did not stop it. We let them fail. Oh man, if there was a spiritual Child Protective Service, they would take Adam and Eve away from us permanently given the lousy job we did.

Father: Oh, you're right! Imagine if the spiritual CPS ever discovered I let a man who had no prior experience have dominion over the earth and be responsible for naming every creature and that I made him a special bride and then put a serpent in there with a tree that would cause them to lose their immortality. What a failure we are.

Jesus: We better go to the Holy Spirit and see if he can give us some anti-depressants until we get past this stage.

Father: You're right. I am so depressed. I do not know what to do with Adam now.

Now I hope you forgive my irreverence, but I trust you all know the above is a ridiculous conversation that never happened. That is not to say that God did not have regrets; in fact, he said, "I regret that I ever made man" (Genesis 6:6). However, we should not think for a moment that our Lord and Savior dwelt in the failure; no, they looked to provide for a future.

Now let me just offer one possibility of what the conversation between the Father and Jesus might have been at the time.

Father and Jesus talking from Context 2: Discussion from God's Context

Father: It grieves my heart to see Adam make that mistake.

Jesus: Yes, I know it does, especially since now you will have to ask them to leave the garden until we can fix this problem so their evil does not become immortal.

Father: You know I love Adam and Eve with my whole being. I created them to be in relationship with me, but the universe I designed and the way I exist force me to separate them from myself forever because of this sin. There is no way out of this, because the result of sin is separation from me, and I cannot stop being the God that I am.

Jesus: There is one way, Father.

Father: I know, but I could not ask you to do that.

Jesus: It is our creation. I will go live with them and die for them so we can be in relationship with them again.

Father: Thank you, Son. I will start preparing the way.

Jesus: Great, Dad. Let's get to work on bringing our children back home.

So, this is what I tell parents: Do not spend much time grieving over your mistakes or your children's mistakes. Instead, look to see what part of your life (attitudes, money, actions, and time) you will have to sacrifice to restore the relationship with your children. You cannot prevent your children from making mistakes or sinning. As a matter of fact, God does not expect you to have children who do not sin. However, he does expect you to love them as he has loved you. This will call for you to lay down your wants, needs, and desires to train them and provide a spiritual heritage for them as he laid down His life for you. God wants us to live in a context that includes hope, restoration, and love; and it is this context that we can allow to guide our actions.

Consider this story of a time when my wife and I saw the same circumstances from different contexts.

STORY 3:
We Are Failures. Maybe Not?

Let me set the stage: It is six o'clock in the morning and I am walking downstairs to shower and prepare for my job. As I walk past the computer, I notice our seventeen-year-old son's biography on the screen. My wife, who homeschools our children, has been working on it. It catches my eye, so I sit down to read it. It is an eleven-page document that lists every course my son has taken and all his accomplishments. Now please bear with me, but I need to list a few of the highlights below so you can get a sense of his accomplishments.

- Third place, regional debate team
- Second place, state debate team
- Second place, Youth in Government state tournament
- Varsity basketball player
- Six weeks as journeyman plumber
- Built an extension on our home
- Over one thousand hours of community service
- Led adult Bible classes with his mother and father
- Chemistry student of the year at the local community college as a high school junior
- Two hundred hours as a certified camp counselor
- 4.0 grade point average
- SAT testing qualified him for a full-ride academic scholarship at local state university

After reading this eleven-page tribute to my son, I was excited and grateful for all my wife did to produce these results. I could not wait for Tracey to wake up so I could acknowledge her for all that she had produced in our son. I went through the shower-shave-and-dress routine just basking in our son's accomplishments.

When I came out of the bathroom, Tracey was sitting at the computer with a rather grim look. Luckily, after being married for twenty-two years, I recognized it was not the time to be enthusiastic and give the "Aren't we wonderful!" husband speech. In years past, I would have just walked up to her and told her how wonderful we are and what a great job we were doing, totally ignoring her mood and her needs. But you only put your foot in your mouth so many times during a marriage before you learn to dislike the taste of Desenex. So, with all the self-control I could muster, I took a seat next to her and said what all wives love to hear their husband ask: "What's wrong, dear?" (Never ask this question unless you're committed to three things: first, that you will listen for at least thirty minutes; second, that you will have to apologize for something; and third, you will not offer any solution until much later.)

Well, the answer to my question was, of course, fairly complicated and lengthy, but the bottom line was, in typing the eleven-page biography, Tracey had realized all the things she had failed to accomplish with our son, especially an intimate relationship with her. She could see all the areas where either apathy or spiritual laziness inhibited her from obtaining these objectives. She made valid points about where we had failed, both individually and together. There were many areas where I could have done better in supporting her in her role as the teacher and mother. There were many areas where she thought she could have done better. The areas where we were weak cost us some of the affinity we believed was possible with our son. Not that we had a bad relationship with him, quite the opposite. Most parents would be jealous of the level of communication that happened between our seventeen-year-old and us. However, the level of affinity was not as deep as we had dreamed and hoped, and we could see that our actions cost us that affinity. We dreamed of being one with our children as Jesus is one with the Father.

Now you can imagine that if you dwell in the context that your actions cost you your relationship with your children, you can reach a very dark level of discouragement and depression, which was where my lovely wife was heading. Of course, being discouraged and depressed around your children reduces the level of communication, which of course, reinforces the depression. You are left in a downward spiral that ends in the death of relationships.

Fortunately, my wife and I chose a different path. That week I was focusing my life on Philippians 4:7-8, which says, "Think upon these things: that which is good, lovely, and of good report, and the peace of God will be with you." My wife was reading a book called *We Still Kiss*. Between her book and my commitment to Phil 4:7-8, we were able to focus on the eleven pages of accomplishment rather than the failures.

This change in the way we talk about our son changes everything. We now walk around the house rejoicing in what God has done through our son. This leads to an appreciation for him, to which he is naturally drawn. The relationship with our son grows deeper, and we are able to prepare together for the upcoming year with a son who knows he is appreciated, and he is preparing with parents who know God is working and who can live with the fact that they have made mistakes.

In conclusion, the two-fold choice before you is whether to recognize the context you currently live from and then to decide whether you want to change it. If you decide to change it, please remember that the old context will persist like the ocean's current: unseen but powerful, it will pull you to dwell on your family's failures. To prevent an ocean's current from pulling you in the wrong direction, you turn on your engines and steer toward a fixed point on the horizon to stay on course. You have the same principle here: *you* must decide to go in a different direction and choose the context that you want your family to live from. Then choose the actions you are going to take based on the context you choose. At first, it will seem your friends and your whole family and friends are working against you because they are comfortable and used to the current drift. It will be hard work to keep your actions consistent with your new context, but after a while, your family and friends will join you because the context you have created gives them a desirable future.

If you take your eye off the goal or stop working hard, the drift of the "self" context will pull you off course. You could start with simple steps such as listing all the accomplishments in your life and your spouse's life, and then move on to listing the things your children have accomplished. Spend the next couple of weeks thanking God in private prayer and consistently acknowledge your family for all of their accomplishments. Out of the blue, say to your daughter, "Remember when you got an A on your first math test? I was so proud." Make the next couple weeks times of encouragement. Your family will call and thank me.

SOMETHING TO CONSIDER
Where can I reveal and express love today?

3

What Difference Would It Make if I Had Intentional and Creative Responses to Circumstances?

Principle: Our automatic response reveals our heart; our intentional, creative response can express our love.

As parents we are always responding to our children. Briefly consider all the areas where our parenting job requires a response

- ❏ Our baby cries; how should we respond?
- ❏ Our child is gifted in music but does not like to practice; how should we respond?
- ❏ Our child is too centered on his appearance; how should we respond?
- ❏ Our child brought home a report card with five As; how should we respond?
- ❏ Our child got caught using drugs at our best friend's house: how should we respond?
- ❏ Our child received the Christian Character award at a national tournament; how should we respond?

- ❑ Our child spends all his money on video games; how should we respond?
- ❑ Both of our children won "Camper of the Year" in the same year; how should we respond?
- ❑ Our younger children are always fighting; how should we respond?
- ❑ We received a note of appreciation from a leader of the church for our child's community service; how should we respond?
- ❑ Our child constantly talks back to his mother; how should we respond?
- ❑ Our child did not make the basketball team; how should we respond?
- ❑ An ex-spouse is saying bad things about us to our child; how should we respond?

Hopefully, as you read through this list, you saw that the times you are responding to circumstances concerning your child are virtually endless. If we are not intentional, most of our responses will be automatic, reactive ones, and they will not mold our children the way we intended. While our *reactive responses* can reveal our heart, our *intentional responses* have a better shot at getting the result we're looking for because they require creativity and thought.

Before we can work on our responses, the first decision to make should be: What characteristics do we want our children to have when we are finished training and disciplining them? When I think about this, I want a child who regularly portrays the fruits of the Spirit:

- Love
- Joy
- Peace
- Patience
- Kindness
- Goodness
- Faithfulness

I also want a child who is able to understand and express the love of God outlined in I Corinthians 13:4-8:

> [4] Love is patient, love is kind. It does not envy, it does not boast, it is not proud. [5] It is not rude, it is not self-seeking, it is not easily angered, and it keeps no record of wrongs. [6] Love does not delight in evil but rejoices with the truth. [7] It always protects, always trusts, always hopes, always perseveres. [8] Love never fails.

If I end up with children who exhibit the fruit of the Spirit and are capable of true love, I will be excited in my old age.

Once you've identified the characteristics you want in your child, you can commit to intentional, creative responses to circumstances that will generate the results you are looking for. Let me share a few of my intentional, creative responses.

While reading these examples, please think about your own current circumstances and start generating intentional, creative solutions. My examples are not answers, because they were generated in the moment to meet a particular need. Instead, these examples may cause the synapses in your brain to go off and help you create your own intentional, creative responses to the circumstances you must react to each day. I already shared my creative response to difficulty in men's dress, but I think another clothing example will help stimulate your thinking.

STORY 4:
To Buy New Clothes or Not?

One day prior to the basketball event, my eldest son came into the living room and announced that he needed new shirts. I calmly looked up from my paper and stated, "You have plenty of shirts in your closet. What is wrong with them?"

He looked at me and rather arrogantly replied, "I need new shirts because the ones in my closet are not good anymore."

In my typical grouchy-dad-trying-to-rest-and-read-the-paper-after-work mode, I marched him into his room, opened his closet, pointed at the shirts, and started yelling at him about how self-centered and stubborn he was, concluding that obviously, with over forty shirts in his closet, he did not need new ones.

He gave me a stone-cold, silent stare that said, "I am so mad at you. You're such an irresponsible parent. How dare you yell at me." Unfortunately, I had not recovered myself yet (more on this in the next chapter), and I literally started pulling the shirts from the closet and throwing them at him. I had totally lost control at that point! There was absolutely no fruit of the Spirit in my being, yet the fruit is what I wanted my kids to exhibit.

Then it happened. In the middle of my anger, a soft voice spoke to my heart. "What are you doing, and what are you teaching him?" Suddenly, and I do mean suddenly, I shut my mouth; I had nothing to say. My son and I stood there staring at each other. I was desperately trying to dispel my anger, and he was just as determined not to let me off the hook. Finally, I received enough grace to speak. I asked him for forgiveness for losing my temper and not listening to what he had to say. He quickly forgave me and told me so. Now, I still believed that he was self-centered and too focused on clothes, so I was not going to buy him shirts just because I got angry. On the other hand, I needed to do something to show him that I was listening to his needs.

By now I was asking myself the question "How can I be creative and intentional here?" Just by asking myself that question, my mood lightened up, and my son saw that sly little grin that comes across my face in these moments. At that point, he knew my wheels were turning and that I would act consistently with the fruit of the Spirit, but I would also come up with a solution that would catch him off guard.

(Now, I believe that my wife was praying in the other room as I was going through this tirade, and I believe her prayers are what allowed God to get through to my heart. This is another principle for another book: "Only one spouse out of control at a time.")

I came up with a solution and offered it to him. We haggled back and forth for a few minutes, and the conversation truly became a fun discussion. After much negotiation, we reached an agreement: He agreed to give away five shirts from his closet, and I agreed to buy him one shirt for every five given away.

He spent the next two hours carefully going through his closet, and he brought me, to my surprise, twenty-five shirts he was willing to give away. Later that week, Tracey took him out to buy his five shirts. This "deal" lived on in the family, and you can imagine how careful we were about our choices. After you give away five shirts to get one a couple of times, the number of shirts in your closet dwindles rapidly until Christmastime when, if you're lucky, Grandma buys you some shirts without asking for five in exchange.

This intentional, creative response showed my son that I was in tune to his need for clothing that he liked; it taught him to value what he had; and it taught me how eager he was to please me when he knew I was listening. You know by my earlier story about the Men's Wearhouse that our conversation about clothes never ended, but I will say that we never fought about clothes again. We both had learned that there are ways to work things out that acknowledge both of our values and needs.

STORY 5:
Service Restores a Relationship

During a ten-year period of our lives, my family and I lived on what we called "The Farm." At one point, it had been our functioning, certified-organic farm, but at this point in the story, it was not really a farm anymore. The property had a main house; a trailer with two bedrooms; and a small, two-bedroom house on blocks in the back. At one point, we were blessed to have some dear friends with seven children stay in the house in the back. Their children were almost the exact ages of our four youngest, and they homeschooled also. As you can imagine, we had our own little community. The simplest way to describe the privilege of this community is that when I came home each night, the ten youngest kids literally would line up in the driveway and, one at a time, run up and jump into my arms to give me a welcome home hug. It was hard to walk into the house grumpy no matter how hard my day was after I was greeted with so many smiling faces.

However, we did have our spats that needed sorting out from time to time. In one incident, my eldest daughter, who was about eight then, had gotten into an argument with the other family's nine-year-old daughter, whom we'll call Shannon. My daughter told Shannon some rather ugly things. My daughter came running into the house telling me how she was mad at Shannon, and she started telling me the whole story. Clearly these two beloved friends were at odds, and something was needed to restore the relationship.

My normal, automatic response would have been to get the two girls together and make each one see her wrongs. I would have them apologize, and then I would talk to Shannon's parents to make sure everything was resolved. On this day, the little, soft voice led me to do something a little more intentional and creative. I looked at my daughter and gently pointed out that what she had said did not exhibit the character that we wanted her to develop. She agreed with me. So I invited her to go to Shannon's house and tell her mom that she would do Shannon's chores that day because of her ugly words. My daughter agreed to do so, and you could actually see a small smile on her face because she could see she was going to have her friend back quickly.

A little later, my daughter came back home, and I asked her how it had gone. She giggled as she told me that as soon as she started the chores—cleaning the kitchen and doing the dishes (a big deal in a family of nine!)—Shannon started helping, and they laughed and listened to music the whole time they were cleaning the kitchen.

Incidentally, these two are still great friends today, even though Shannon's family eventually moved two thousand miles away.

The intentional, creative response to this little dispute created more friendship than I could have asked for, and it did so quickly. I encourage you not to be in "remote control" mode when your children come to you with problems or questions. Look to see if the Spirit will lead you to an idea you never would have considered before.

STORY 6:

Restitution Was an Important Communication from a Son to a Mom

I work as a financial officer for a management-consulting firm. During this particular stage of my marriage, I traveled frequently during the week and usually flew back into town late on Friday afternoon. My wife would describe me during this stage of our life as a dedicated man who was simply too exhausted to deal with the day-to-day troubles of raising six children. Therefore, she took it upon herself not only to do the cooking, the cleaning, the disciplining, and the homeschooling but also to ensure that there was peace in the house when I finally did get home on Friday nights.

However, one Friday night I walked into the house after driving home from the airport, and there was not the expected peace; the tension in the house was extremely high. The boys were in their shared room, and Mom was busy cleaning stuff (in my house, cleaning late at night is a message that something is wrong). I gave a weak and hesitant "Hi, dear," not knowing what would come my way. I was not ready to ask her what was wrong yet (remember the three things to be ready for if you are going to ask your spouse what is wrong), so I took my suitcase into our room and started changing my clothes.

Well, she followed me into the room, and I knew that was a bad sign. I readied myself to give up my thirty minutes, apologize for something, and hold off on advice until she was done. She then explained to me how difficult one of our sons had been all week. He had flatly refused to do what she'd asked of him that day (it was some mundane chore, nothing unusual). I then heard how she had spent the whole day upset with our son, had gotten nothing done, and now was feeling sick from being upset all day. Then she gave me the X-ray stare that said, "What are you going to do about this? He's *your* son. He learns disrespect from you, so do something!"

After assuring her that I was as upset about this as she was (actually, I was more upset than she was, because being upset did not let me go to bed right away, but saying that probably would not have been wise at the time), I pronounced boldly that I would go forth and talk to the boy.

I marched into my son's room, asked the other two boys to leave, and shut the door behind them. I sat on the floor while my son sat on his bed folding his clothes like nothing was wrong and he had no idea why I was in his room. Fortunately, this was one of those times when I did not have to lose my temper before I heard that soft voice encourage me to communicate with the fruit of the Spirit. Also fortunately, my son was in the proper spirit as well and was willing to have a discussion about what had happened. We had a long discussion about my son being a Christian. I reminded him that being a Christian was *his* profession, not mine, and I pointed out that my job as his father was to assist him in living the way a Christian man should live. He finally acknowledged that he was out of line and owed his mother an apology.

Here is where I could have made the classic mistake of sending him to his mom to apologize. I was fully aware there was more at stake here than just his rebellion of the day. My wife needed to know that I understood her feelings, that she had lost a whole day of her life, and that she had even lost part of her health over this rebellion. When you examine the root of it, you find the same grief that God has when we sin. My wife was grieving that her son would treat her this way, and she grieved over this apparent sign she was losing him.

Given all this, an apology would not suffice; my son needed to do more. So, I discussed with him how his action caused her to lose a whole day and that she was offended but that, more than that, she was hurt. We brainstormed for a few minutes, and we decided that after he apologized for his behavior, he would wash and wax the living room, kitchen, and dining room floors (about a four-hour job) to acknowledge that he'd stolen her time and attempt to compensate for it.

By reminding my son of his values and his desire to follow Christ and to operate consistently with the fruit of the Spirit, I ensured he experienced his action as a gift to his mother rather than as a punishment he was receiving because his mother was mad. While making sure he understood and embraced this concept made the conversation longer than I wanted it to be, it was critical to prevent further resentment. I could not send him back to his mother with this offer to clean and wash the floors unless he could do it with a repentant and joyful heart.

Well, she graciously accepted his apology and the restitution he offered, and he performed the chores admirably. This intentional, creative response, as you can see, allowed my son to learn not only the restitution principle but also restoration. His actions needed to restore the relationship, and an apology, in these circumstances, would not have been enough.

STORY 7:
Mercy for a Liar

Over the years, we have had more than a dozen single mothers live with us until they could get their lives stabilized, or until they could not stand us and our rules.

Our rules for these mothers always included things like being home by ten o'clock, saving half of their income, performing household chores, working toward a goal, and not drinking or using drugs on the property. After each girl moved out, Tracey and I would discuss how it went, and we would review the rules and discuss how they'd worked. After these discussions, there was always one consistent theme: we should have been stricter on the front end so we could show mercy rather than judgment. We found it was easier to have very tough rules and choose when we wanted to have mercy or relax the rules rather than start with lenient rules and then make them stricter later on based on circumstances. We also noticed that the ladies would often lie to avoid the consequences of the rules, and given their life circumstances, most of them were pretty good liars.

During one of these reviews with Tracey, we decided on a new rule: the ladies were granted one "free" lie to us. However, if they were caught in a second lie, they would be asked to leave. Now this was a very strict rule for us. We never had a rule that if they violated it, they would have to leave. If they were late for curfew, we simply talked to them; if they got caught doing drugs, we put further restrictions on them, but even then, we did not ask them to leave. However, after some discussion, we agreed this would be part of our rules.

So, before each girl moved in, we would lay out all the rules, spending extra time on the "no lying" rule. We assured them that we knew they lied habitually because it was inherent in people who had burned up all their family relationships. Also, many of these ladies had drug or alcohol problems, which usually contributed to developing lying habits. We assured them that we loved them even though they were liars, but that starting then, they were going to tell the truth. We then explained that the first lie would be "free," and after that, the consequences would be grim: we would ask them to leave.

Well, one lady (who will remain nameless) moved in with her baby. She was passionate and enthusiastic, but she was also very much in pain, and she relieved that pain by lashing out at Tracey or me. However, we still managed to exhibit the fruit of the Spirit, and we definitely believed God was working in her life while she was in our home. After she had been with us for a couple of months, I caught her in a lie about where she was going. I confronted her about it and let her know she had used up her free lie.

About a month later, I found out that she had lied to me again; it was about something trivial, but it was lie. (The problem with habitual lying is that you lie about things unnecessarily; lying becomes a reaction to any question from an authority.) I told Tracey what had happened, and we were both grieved—not because we were offended by her lying to us but because we were going to ask this lady, on whom God was clearly working, to leave our home.

Neither of us wanted to ask her to leave, yet neither of us wanted to abandon our stand on lying. Then that soft voice prodded us again to "be creative, be intentional; after all, God used a donkey to talk to some people." That smile I told you about came to my face as I began looking for a way to use this circumstance to honor, value, and build character in this woman.

Ultimately, Tracey and I came up with a solution: I planned to tell her that if she confessed the lie to me, we would not invoke the rule of asking her to leave. The creative part was that I would not tell her which lie I knew about. Bear in mind that the lie was about something so trivial that I don't even remember what it was now.

I was excited; we'd found a creative way to deal with this circumstance, and it would force our friend to face her sin while showing her mercy. She came home that evening, and I asked her to sit on the couch with me. Tracey sat across the room. I explained my discovery to her: I knew she had lied to me, and our rule would force me to ask her to leave. She started to cry. She was very upset because while she was failing in some areas, she was making great progress with the Lord in other areas. I then made my offer: she could stay if she confessed the lie without me telling her what it was. A worried but curious look came over her face. Before the incident, she'd already suspected that somehow I knew things, and she couldn't figure out how I knew them. She always believed that somehow God spoke to Tracey regularly through circumstances, so she had no idea what we knew.

The conversation lasted an hour. She confessed things that she had done while living with us that we'd had no idea about. She said, "Well, I lied when I said I never did drugs on the property. I smoked marijuana behind the trailer two months ago."

I smiled and said, "Nope, that's not the lie I know about."

She went on and on; she must have confessed twenty things Tracey and I hadn't known about, although she never did confess the trivial matter I knew about because she had forgotten it.

After her confessions, Tracey and I hugged her and thanked her for her honesty and told her she was welcome to stay. We worked out a few extra restrictions, as you can imagine, but the relationship continues to this day.

You can see how the intentional, creative solution Tracey and I came up with allowed this young lady to clear her conscience and, most importantly, feel our unconditional love. I do not know if we could have contrived a better way for her to learn that God loved her no matter what she had done; He only asked that she talk to Him.

In my house, we also use many of the ordinary ways of disciplining, such as time-outs and taking away driving privileges or computer time. At the same time, all my children start to worry when that little grin comes across my face and I say, "Now you don't want me to start thinking up creative ways to respond to this circumstance, do you?"

As I mentioned at beginning of this chapter, our opportunities to respond intentionally or creatively are endless. We have to deal with self-centered children, fights among our children and their friends, acts of defiance, and people who outright lie to us. These are all opportunities for us to demonstrate that we can express the fruit of the Spirit in all circumstances. However, to do this, we must acknowledge it is the Spirit that lives within us that allows us to respond, rather than our own self-control or willpower.

SOMETHING TO CONSIDER

What circumstances in your life today call for an intentional, creative response?

4

Recovering Yourself: Can You Be Who You Say You Are?

Principle: Asking someone to recover who they say they are is an effective tool.

Your life as a parent gets easier once your children have made the decision to be baptized and to follow Christ. Once your young person declares to the universe that they will lay down their lives and follow Christ, you no longer have to push your children; you can point your children in the direction they have chosen.

At this point in their lives, my children have come to know the phrase "Recover yourself." When I say, "Recover yourself," to my children, I am telling them to recover who *they* say they are. I am not asking them to live up to my or even God's expectations; I am asking them to live up to their *own* expectations. Once you embrace this concept, you can have conversations with your kids that call them to a future they desire, rather than convincing them to embrace the future you desire for them. You are no longer telling them who they should be. Instead, you are inviting them to be who *they* want to be.

When I first started having this conversation with my kids, I noticed one of my children in particular took days to recover himself. Even after he heard my "brilliant" speech about who *he* says he is and how *he* is the one who pronounced Christ as his Lord (so many brilliant words), it still took days for him to recover himself.

In the beginning, this frustrated Tracey and me. Then we decided to refine the conversation to talk about reducing the amount of time it took him to recover himself. This took the pressure for an immediate response off of him and reminded him that he could succeed in recovering himself if he gave himself time. It also allowed me to praise him when he could recover himself in one day instead of three. After about a year, he had his recovery time down to hours. Now, about seven years later, his recovery time is often down to minutes. This approach allowed Tracey and me to have patience during the times he was angry. At the same time, we encouraged him to live out his faith by exhibiting the fruit of the Spirit, because that is who he said he wanted to be. We were able to keep the judgment toward his inappropriate behavior out of our voices by focusing on who he said he was, and this allowed him to hear our challenge to recover himself.

It is so encouraging for your children to know that when they are not behaving consistently with who Christ asks them to be, your response is acknowledgment, not judgment:

- You acknowledge that they are Christians.
- You acknowledge that they are mature enough to have their own standards.
- You acknowledge that they are fully capable of living up to their own standards.
- You acknowledge that we all fall, and they are capable of getting up.

This is a very simple conversation on the surface, but please spend some time thinking about who you say you are when you say you are a Christian.

Where do you need to recover yourself? When you recover yourself, God can use you to ask your children where they need to recover themselves. At that point, their recovery will happen not because you want it or because God asks them to recover but because this is who your children have claimed they are.

STORY 8:
An Athlete Develops a Strong Ability to Recover Herself

When my youngest son graduated high school and went to college to get an education and play basketball, I switched from coaching boys' varsity basketball to coaching my daughter's varsity basketball team.

As a new coach for these young ladies, I made it a point to discover their dreams. Four or five of them were seniors (my daughter was a freshman at the time), and naturally they were apprehensive about this new coach who had only coached boys before. I had been warned that coaching girls was different, and these girls were intense on and off the court. I needed to figure out if coaching boys was different than coaching girls. What I realized was one thing was not different: my job was to coach them to become the players and team they wanted to be.

I spent the first couple practices working with them to discover who they said they were. It was easy to see one young lady clearly wanted to play basketball at the next level in college. She was one of our best players, but I had heard she also had a tendency to fly off the handle from time to time. My opportunity arose at practice. I am still not sure why, but during that practice, she angrily ran out of the gym and holed up in the girls' bathroom.

When this happened, every player froze and waited to see what I would do, I had a reputation of being strict and loud. I stayed with the team for a few minutes as they practiced, and then I told the players to keep doing their drills. I walked down the hall to the girls' restroom, knocked, and said through the door, "You have ten minutes to recover yourself to be the kind of player you have told me you want to be," and then I went back to practice. Ten minutes later, she came out with her emotions under control, and we continued practice. This created a way for us to work together as coach and player. For the rest of the year, I continued to clarify who she wanted to be and to point her toward her own goal. For her work, she ended up getting a full basketball scholarship to college.

STORY 9:
Exploring Foundational Beliefs to Discover Who People Say They Are

Over the years, because of the people who lived with us and because of our work in the church, Tracey and I were often asked to talk with people and see if we could help them.

Once, we were asked to talk with a young couple with two children. The couple separated on and off and had drug and alcohol problems. We had not worked with the couple before, so I was not familiar with who they said they were. Below is the conversation I had with them after we got past "Hello." I'll call the husband Matt and the wife Melody.

Don: So, Matt, I am sure you have heard that Tracey and I are Christians.
Matt: Yup.
(Melody nodded her head in agreement.)
Don: Well, to make matters clear, Tracey and I are more than willing to see if we can help you and Melody sort things out, but you need to know all of our advice will come from our interpretation of the Bible and its teaching.
Matt: Figured that. No problem.
Don: Well, before I start giving any advice, I was wondering if you could speak a little about what you use for your foundational beliefs when you are calm and centered.
Matt: Not sure what you mean.
Don: Well, for example, one biblical principle is that a man should love his wife like Christ loved the church. I translate that to mean that you should put aside your needs and desires to serve your wife's needs and desires.

So if I were counseling you, I would use this principle, but you might not agree with it.

Matt: Well, to tell you the truth, no, not all the time. I do not agree with all the things the Bible says.

Don: OK, great. That is what I was looking for. I want to see what you do agree with and where you derive your principles from. Melody, what about you? Where do you get your principles from?

Melody: Well, I am similar to Matt. I don't agree with the Bible, so I create my own principles based on my beliefs.

Don: Thank you for sharing. Matt, what about you then, do you make up your own principles based on circumstances, prior history, and personal beliefs?

Matt: Yeah, I think that's right. Never thought about it that way before, but that is right.

Don: Thank you both for helping me clarify where your principles are derived from. Now I know how to have a conversation with you.

Matt: What do you mean?

Don: Well, my guess is that you do not have your principles written down anywhere, and since you make them up based on the circumstances at hand, you might not even have them articulated orally yet.

Matt: So?

Don: Well, as we work together, we'll need to identify your principles, then identify Melody's principles and see where they are common and where they're different. I am not talking about when things are bad and you're angry or drunk. I am talking about the principles you want to live by. We will need to create those.

Melody: Why?

Don: Because if we use my principles that I do my best to base on the Bible, they might not be consistent with yours. We need to identify and articulate your principles so that when times go bad, we can call on both of you to live by those principles.

The rest of our counseling sessions were difficult and long because, before tackling each issue, we had to back up and discover the underlying principles from which this couple was willing to work. We did make progress, but it was slow. However, we would have made much less progress if I had insisted on instilling my principles in their lives. As a matter of fact, the counseling probably would have ended after the first session. You can see how this approach allows you to counsel someone from any faith, or even from agnosticism or atheism.

STORY 10:
Recovering Joy

My youngest son, Joey, always loved basketball and played it with great joy and enthusiasm. His goal was to play at a high level in high school and then go on to play in college.

In the fall of his senior year, due to injuries and visits to colleges for tryouts, it appeared his dreams were not going to be fulfilled, and I watched the joy leave his game as the dream appeared to die. In January, I remembered the principle of recovering yourself. So I sat down with Joey, and we had a number of discussions about recovering who he said he was. Joey remembered that he started this journey as a joyful and content person, and these qualities were things he did not want to lose. To his credit, Joey was able to examine the circumstance, change his heart, and play with joy, even knowing the dream might not come true.

To this day, I believe that if I had yelled at him or nagged him about how he needed to be joyful, his season would have ended in misery. Instead, I invited him to consider that living with joy in the pursuit of a dream—even if it fails—is more important than actually obtaining the dream. (To see how the season ended, read the last chapter.)

STORY 11:
Called to Be Content

My daughter Annie was a camp counselor at Camp Good News. During her second year, she was going to be a counselor for five weeks. As she tells the story, when she arrived for the first week, the trainers informed the junior counselors that doing the dishes for the summer would teach them a lesson in service. Annie was disheartened to think she would spend five weeks doing dishes for hundreds of kids. She and the other counselors were quite grumpy about this, and plenty of grousing ensued. By Wednesday, Annie believed that, in her quiet time, a soft voice was telling her to be content in all things. She listened to the soft voice and took its message to heart. The next morning, she took on changing her attitude and the attitude of her peers; by the end of the week, she had recovered her joy. When she returned for the second week, the camp counselors announced that she was relieved of kitchen duty. This was a heartfelt lesson for Annie.

When camp was over, Annie announced to all of her friends, her family, and her teammates that she had learned to be content in everything and that for the rest of her life, she was going to live from that principle. From that day on, when things were not going her way, I was careful to gently prod her toward her own declaration. If her mom or I asked her to do something against her wishes and she responded negatively, I simply asked her if she was living from the principle she had embraced, and she always responded well. When some of her friends gossiped about her and said wicked, untrue things about her, we talked about her decision to be content, and it helped her talk to her friends in a manner that served rather than confronted them. I suspect that for years to come, my job in helping Annie be more like Christ will be easy as long as I remember who she said she wanted to be and put aside who I think she should be.

Before you decide to start calling your children to be who they say they are, it is advisable to think through who you say you are. Then the next time you behave inconsistently with your values, intentionally recover yourself. Notice how long it takes you to recover yourself. Over time, see if you can expedite your recovery. When you have developed the muscle of recovering yourself, it is time to work with your children.

SOMETHING TO CONSIDER

Are you asking people to be who you think they should be or who they say they want to be?

5

Can You Live Your Life from the Perspective That "You're Wrong until Proven Otherwise?"

Principle: Consider that the first step in any circumstance is to examine yourself (look for the beam in your own eye) so that you will be able to clearly see the appropriate response.

One key principle of relationships that Christ points out is the idea that you're wrong until proven otherwise. I will admit that this is a strange wording of the verse that says, "Before you criticize your brother, take the beam out of your own eye" Matthew 7:3-5. I know many adults do not understand this principle, but even those who do understand it seem to behave as though it does not apply to dealing with our children. When something goes wrong, we immediately move to correct and discipline them. Consider that, by doing so, we miss the critical step that Christ knows is necessary for healthy relationships. We must first examine our own "eyes" before we can discipline our children.

This principle is a great supplement to the ideas presented in chapter 3 about creating intentional, creative responses to all circumstances.

Our reactive responses often create more problems than they resolve because we are blinded to our faults or responsibility in the matter. Our chance of creating an effective response is increased dramatically if we can see our behavior clearly from our children's perspective.

STORY 12:
Acknowledging the Log in My Eye Allows Son to Hear and Speak

One of my sons was seventeen years old and in his senior year of high school. We were homeschooling him, and he decided that he wanted to attend Rice University. This required him to score 1400 on the SAT test, which was about one hundred points higher than he'd scored on a practice test. Being the brilliant and supportive father that I am, I asked Tracey to sign him up for an SAT preparatory course that ran three hours a day from Friday through Sunday for five weeks. It cost $600. When we signed him up for it, he expressed his doubts about whether he could handle this with all the other work he was doing. I reviewed his schedule with him in great detail and showed him that he had two hours of free time a day, even with a generous allotment of nine hours of sleep and three hours for eating. I went over each class, and I pointed out how sacrificing free time would give him time to attend and do well in class. After this overwhelmingly rational argument, I convinced him that he could and should take the class.

Weekend one went by without a hitch. As weekend two approached, I asked him if he had studying to do, and he mentioned some study words. We studied those words together, and I started telling him that I wanted him to write sentences for each word he got wrong. He resisted this idea. Without saying it, he was telling me, "We planned the weekend classes—we did not plan on me studying for those classes, and I am not going to do it." On Saturday night of that second weekend, I looked through the SAT workbook and found blank pages in sections that I knew they'd covered. In my head, I heard the little voice saying, "He is not doing his best. I spent a lot of money so this boy can have some choices; he needs to do his best. I am going to let him go to church in the morning and to his class and to his Sunday-night Bible study, but when he gets home, I'm going to nail him. I will keep it pleasant and tell him what I want."

Notice that in this one-sided mental conversation, I was not thinking, "Dang, I forgot to talk to him about my expectations for the course; I forgot to put in scheduled study time when I convinced him to attend the course; and I forgot to create a strategy for the course. I better figure out a way to make this work for him given it was my idea, not his." Most of all, I forgot the principle, outlined in chapter 4 about calling our children to be who they want to be rather than who we want them to be.

I now had a choice: I could take the position that he should try his best, or I could start from the position that I'd forgotten to set up clear expectations when I'd asked him to take the course and see if my mistake could be corrected. I stuck with the first conversation.

When he came home from his Bible study with his younger brother, we chatted briefly, and then I asked him to bring me his SAT workbook. Not suspecting that he was about to get hammered, he went to the car, got his workbook, and sat down next to me on the couch. His mother sat in a chair in the same room, and his brother was on the other couch. I flipped to the geometry section, showed him the blank pages, and pointed at a page that looked like it contained a problem.

I said, "How come you did not do this problem?" My voice had a curt, accusatory tone.

He replied testily, "Because it's not a problem, Dad. Look at it—it's just a formula we reviewed in class."

Well, I was not going to let him outtalk me, so I searched a bit more carefully and flipped to some pages that I knew had half-finished problems. Now my voice was a little louder and much more curt (tip: if you start getting rude, you're probably defending a weak position), and I said, "Well, what about these problems? I am sending you to this class to do well, not just get by. You need to do these problems."

His voice grew more agitated, and he said, "We do this workbook in class, and I wrote out the problems we did; I am not doing those problems."

Another tip: If Dad is going down an angry spiral, the best way to accelerate that is to tell him, "I am not…" In the stern, I-am-the-dad voice, I said, "I do not care what you think; I am telling you to do them."

He continued talking to me, but now his face was crunched up, and his eyes were fixed on me with a stare that said, "You. Cannot. Make. Me." He managed to say, "I am going to take some of the practice tests; that is what I am going to do."

I responded quickly, "Well, then, let me see *that* book." He left and returned with the practice book.

I relaxed a little and started working myself toward enrolling him instead of forcing him, but it was too late for that now.

He returned and handed me the practice textbook, and to his dismay, we discovered that it had more than practice tests in it. There were also reading assignments on each subject area covered in the class.

I suggested that he needed to create a plan for his reading, practice tests, and word study. I was being very enrolling. However, he had dug his trench a little deeper as he sat next to me in a defiant posture that said, "Go ahead. Be a jerk. I am not doing it." I flipped through the chapters and showed him that the book had only ninety pages. He could read that in two hours. He sat in his I-will-not-speak mode.

I tried a softer and kinder tone to enroll him in the idea that this class was for his own good. I gave my relationship-building speech, and he responded with silence.

I tried kidding around with him, saying, "Come on, we're wasting more time with you being mad than if you just did the work."

He raised his eyebrows and muttered the all-powerful monosyllable: "So?"

I phased from Hyde to Jekyll and back to Hyde. I exploded. Jumping up from the couch, I yelled, "I do not have to put up with this behavior! How dare you go to your Bible study and come home and behave like this!" I stormed upstairs before I said something really stupid. Halfway up the stairs, I decided to go back down and tell him, "You are in rebellion and in sin!" and then I went to bed. It took me a while, but I finally slept, knowing that somehow I would fix this in the morning.

Morning came, and it was on my mind that my relationship with my son, which had been stellar, had blown up the night before. Standing in the shower, letting the hot water massage my back, an idea came to mind: I was angry because I considered my son to be my friend, and he did not treat me like a friend. While I was still his father, we were moving toward friendship, and I expected different behavior from him. A friend would never treat me that way. Now, I believed, I had a way to talk to him about this in a healthier manner.

In case you have not noticed, I had completely forgotten the "log" principle; I was still looking at his behavior and ignoring my own.

I woke the boys up. While they were getting up, I noticed the SAT books were open on the table. Obviously my son had stayed up and completed a lot of work. The boys came to the couch for prayer, and we prayed with Mom. I then asked my son to come to the giant master bathroom that I call my office.

He sat on the edge of the tub with a softened look, but still, right below the softness, was the stare, ready to pop out. I told him, "You know, son, I thought a lot about last night, and I do not want to get angry like that. It was not appropriate for me to get angry. I thought a lot about what got me upset, and the problem is, son, I consider you to be my friend. We are moving from a father-director relationship to a father-advisor and friend relationship. Really, as my friend, I do not expect you to give me the silent, sarcastic attitude. I hope that we can talk things out and brainstorm a solution together. That is the relationship I want."

I said all of this in a calm, sincere manner. However, I was bewildered because normally when I spoke like this, he honored my attempts and confessed his own wrongs. We would hug, and it would be beautiful. This time, his face tightened; the stare was back, and his lips curled. The lip-curling thing meant he wanted to say something to me; it would not be nice, and he would communicate it only if he thought I would respond properly. I was about to leave when I realized he was going to talk, so I leaned back on the sink. He said, "Dad, if you want to talk like friends, then you cannot just tell me, 'I do not care what you think; you're going to do it.' As soon as you said that, Dad, I thought, 'Whatever,' and decided there was no point in talking with you anymore."

Well, fortunately, my heart was still soft enough to see that he was right. The very thing I was asking him to do—to be my friend—I was not doing. What a hypocrite! I immediately apologized.

We then had an actual conversation, and in three minutes, we created an agreement that he would design a study plan that would cover his weak areas. In any area where he was getting an acceptable score, there would be no reason for him to study. He smiled; we agreed with the plan. Both of our hearts were now released from anger. I went to work with joy, and he went to do his work without being angry at his dad. He went on to score a 1470 on his SAT.

This long, drawn-out process had been unnecessary. If I had started with "What did I miss?" rather than "He is not trying his best," the first conversation would have been very different. It cost me an extra hour or two of time and a night's peaceful sleep. However, I will say that it is delightful to have a son with whom I can work out such difficulties in less than twenty-four hours.

I would rather not humiliate myself with more stories for you to get this point. However, I could relate countless stories of parents that I have counseled who said their children would not talk to them. The following is one example of a conversation I had with a friend of mine and his son.

STORY 13:
The Trap a Son Sets for His Father

"Joe" came to me for help with his son, but we began by meeting alone. He explained his concerns to me, saying, "My kid is disrespectful; he never talks to me politely, and he doesn't listen to me."

I've heard this complaint often, so I said, "Really? That's too bad. Have you tried getting him alone when you're not upset and just reasoning with him?"

Joe said, "Yeah, I have taken him to dinner twice, and he just sits there and grunts or shakes his head." Asked how his son was doing otherwise, Joe told me, "His grades are slipping. He stays up late and gets up late, does not do his chores, and spends most of his time with his friends." I asked Joe what his son, Frank, thought of me and whether he thought Frank might trust me. Joe responded, "Well, I am not sure. I think you intimidate him a little, but he trusts you."

I suggested that Joe invite Frank to lunch, which I would also attend, and tell him that I was there to help the two of them communicate. Joe said, "OK. It won't make any difference, but I will try it."

A week later, I sat in a booth at a Denny's restaurant waiting for Joe and Frank. They arrived and sat across from me. They both had apprehensive looks on their faces, and I knew we would need God's grace.

I started by saying, "Well, we are here today, Frank, because your dad has a concern about your behavior and thinks all communication between you two has stopped. Before we get started, I have one question for both of you: Do you love each other?"

They both had startled looks. They were caught off guard with this very practical but confronting question. I do not think they had considered this before. (Chapter 4 was about recovering yourself. By starting with this question, I was able to discover the foundation I would be working on and refer back to their answers later.)

Frank said, "Yeah."

Joe blurted, "Yes, of course I love my son."

I told them this was great, and I added, "We now have a solid foundation to work on, but before we get going, why don't you make eye contact and tell each other that you love each other."

Dad went first and told Frank that he loved him. Frank turned toward his dad, looked him in the eye, and told his father that he loved him.

Now, if I had been smart, I would have ended the meeting right there because it was clear that before this moment, Joe had been questioning whether his son loved him, and there in that moment his son had created a breakthrough and communicated with his dad. But as you guessed, I was not that smart, and we continued.

Instead, I said, "OK, Joe, why don't you start and speak about your concern about Frank's math class?"

While Joe looked only at me, he began, "Well, he just will not study, and his grades are falling. He is just being lazy and blames it on his teacher. He is a bad example to his brothers and sisters, and he ignores his mother when she tells him to study, and he..." Joe continued on for about five minutes. He then turned to Frank and said, "What do you have to say for yourself, son?"

Frank had a pleasant look on his face; there was no smile but also no hard stare like my family uses. He said nothing.

Joe waited about six seconds and then jumped in with, "I told you he would not talk; he is just in rebellion, and his life is going to be a mess, and..."

I stopped him with, "Joe, hold on a second. Let Frank respond here. Frank, tell your dad what is going on with your math class."

Frank was dead silent. He was not angry or even smart-alecky, just silent with a pleasant facial expression as though he was getting some satisfaction out of the encounter.

Joe waited thirty seconds this time and then began again, "See, he just won't talk, he does not want to work..."

I gently reached across the table, put my hand on Joe's chest, and said, "Wait, Joe, let's let Frank talk. You're both in this dance! You talk; he is silent. You jump in and say some more, and things spiral out of control. Now, Frank, tell me what is going on with your dad and math."

Frank was silent, but this time I had my hand on Joe's chest, actually pushing on him to be quiet. Frank continued in silence, but he grew a little antsy. I looked down at my watch. We waited six minutes—an eternity of silence—and finally Frank said, "He doesn't listen to me. He just lectures me and yells at me. I find it's easier not to talk because then the lecture ends sooner. If I say anything, he just tells me that I am wrong and gives me another lecture, and my math teacher—"

Joe interrupted with, "See? There he goes blaming his math teacher again. If he would just do his work, I would not have to lecture him. It's just ridiculous that he would blame his math teacher, and that is why his mother and I are constantly riding his butt..." He went on for another five minutes.

Frank just looked at me, smiled, and said nothing.

Well, I am not going to type the rest of the two-hour discussion, but you can see where I had to take them. I had to show Joe that he was in a dance with his son, and he was reacting to his son rather than talking with him. At the same time, I had to show Frank that he was baiting his father with his silence, and that he knew what he was doing.

The father needed to see that he had a log in his own eye, and his son was not going to listen until he removed it. Joe's log was that he failed to live by the principle described in James 1:19: "Be slow to speak and quick to listen." If the father wanted to shift things, he was going to have to remove this log, apologize for years of not listening, and start listening. Frank, on the other hand, could have taken the initiative on his side and removed his log. He did not live by the principles of Exodus 20:12 and Ephesians 6:1–3: he did not honor his mother and father. I promised a breakthrough in the relationship if either one of them focused on removing his own log.

All parents are faced with this dilemma when they start losing the relationships they have with their children. The key is not the child; the key is the relationship parents have with their Heavenly Father and how well they allow the Holy Spirit to point out the logs. Now, even after we see the logs, we have to develop skills in communication, but the first step is log removal.

While taking responsibility for your own "logs," be careful not to fall into the trap of thinking you're a failure. I was not asking this father to examine his past and beat himself up because he failed with Frank. We have already covered the idea of context: we must look from the future that God promises us. It is looking from the future of forgiveness and wholeness that makes removing the log a joy rather than the first step toward antidepressants. Seeing a log in your eye is a communication that God is speaking to you. It means you are in relationship with the Creator of the universe. We must constantly remove logs so that, with clear eyes, we can see what needs to be removed from our children's eyes so that they can see. Otherwise, we just keep poking our children in the eyes because we do not see clearly.

The final outcome of this story is encouraging. I talk sometimes to the son, who is now in his thirties, and he has a high regard for his dad. They do joint projects together, and their communication is growing every year, demonstrating God's grace rather eloquently.

Now, I cannot end this section without giving you some tools for removing logs and clearing your conscience. The Peace Maker[1] materials and principles are easy to understand and consistent with biblical concepts. You can find these concepts at HisPeace.org. Allow me to share two principles from Peace Makers.

THE SEVEN AS OF CONFESSION

1. Address everyone involved (all those whom you affected).
2. Avoid "if," "but," and "maybe" (do not try to excuse your wrongs).
3. Admit specifically (both attitudes and actions).
4. Acknowledge the hurt (express sorrow for hurting someone).
5. Accept the consequences (such as making restitution).
6. Alter your behavior (change your attitudes and actions).
7. Ask for forgiveness.

I strongly urge you to consider these when you "clean up" wrongs with your kids.

---

1   Ken Sande, *The Peace Maker* (Baker Publishing Group, 2004).

THE FOUR PROMISES OF FORGIVENESS

1. I will not dwell on this incident.
2. I will not bring up this incident again and use it against you.
3. I will not talk to others about this incident.
4. I will not let this incident stand between us or hinder our personal relationship.

I suggest parents consider these promises as they tell their kids that they forgive them.

When trying any new principles, consider taking the perspective of an athlete who is learning new skills. Tell yourself: I will master these principles through practice and learning from failure. You will discover new insights each time you try to utilize these principles.

The last thing I will say about the principle that "You're wrong until proven otherwise" is that this is a one-way street—you must learn it first. This is not something you teach your children or spouse in the middle of an upset. After you have lived this way for six months, encountering every circumstance with self-reflection before poking around in others' eyes, then you can attempt to teach your children and spouse what you have been doing. Attempting to teach this principle before you have mastered it is a severe poke in the other person's eye; if you do this, be prepared to have your finger chopped off.

SOMETHING TO CONSIDER

If they are not listening to you, maybe you are not hearing them.

6

What Does It Mean to Lay Down Your Life?

Principle: Laying down our lives for our kids means giving them what they need spiritually and emotionally, from the depths of our souls, not our pocketbooks.

The reason we live and breathe with a hope of heaven is because Christ laid down his life for us. He is the example to all parents of how to take care of our children. This idea really constitutes the heart of this book. Every principle written here calls you to sacrifice yourself in some way for your children's physical, emotional, and, ultimately, spiritual well-being. We must set ourselves aside—even when we are right and our children, friends, or parents are wrong—if we want to have rich, rewarding relationships with the people we love.

Many modern, middle-class parents would say they have sacrificed everything for their children, but their children still left the church and are not following the Lord. The relationships between these parents and their children are strained. The parents resent that they provided everything for their kids and the kids never appreciated it. However, if you asked these parents what they have done for their children, you might get a list like this:

- I paid for a private school.
- I paid for their college with my retirement money.
- I drove them to band practice every night.
- I bought instruments and sports equipment.
- I attended all their sporting events since they were five, which is approximately 433 games, 1,500 hours, and 220 gallons of gas.
- When they were sixteen, I bought them brand-new cars.
- I took them to church every weekend.

I'm sure there's an inexhaustible list of the sacrifices parents make for their children. The items in the list above are wonderful gifts, but they have little to do with laying down your life for your children. Contrast that list with Christ's behavior toward those for whom he accepted earthly responsibility. When Christ came to earth, he picked his twelve closest friends and did the following for them:

- He gave them no place to lay their heads.
- He promised them that they would suffer for him.
- He took them away from their families.
- He had them eat from other people's fields
- He had them journey by foot as poor men for long periods of time.
- He made them sit through countless lectures.

However, his disciples followed him until their own deaths. He gave them almost nothing materially—just the bare necessities—yet they loved him. He provided them with the following:

- His undivided attention, except when they knew he was alone and praying to his Father

- An example of how to serve the world through passion and mercy
- The ability to confront hypocrisy
- His wisdom
- Predictions of their failures, yet promises that He had a place prepared for them
- A teacher's heart that entertained and encouraged difficult questions
- The supreme example of giving His life while showing love toward His enemies
- Rising from death, as promised
- Prayer for them to be one
- A challenge for them to teach others
- Instructions for reaching the world
- Allowance for their failure without judgment

This is not to say there is anything wrong with providing your children gifts, driving them around, taking them to sports, and giving them cars. Let's just not mistake this for laying down our lives for our kids.

STORY 14:
Allowing Your Child to Experience Pain

When one of my daughters was sixteen, a young man approached me and asked for permission to call her on the phone. (Yes, we are strict. Boys even had to get permission to call.) I knew and liked the young man a lot, and my daughter was interested in taking his calls. However, I believed that at her age, this would only lead to a more serious relationship and stronger emotional ties. Given their age, they could not act on those stronger emotional feelings, so there was a strong likelihood that, if I allowed this, it would end in pain for both of them. From my daughter's point of view, she wanted to do this, had her own justifications, and said that she disagreed with me and that she was willing to risk the future pain.

Frankly, it would have been easy to ignore my daughter's opinions and desires, count on her love for me and her considerable maturity, and just tell the boy no. I knew that if I did this, my daughter and I would still have a fine relationship. That would have been easier on me; it would have been what I wanted to do; and it would even have been what I considered to be the right choice for her. It would have required one conversation with the boy and maybe three or four conversations with my daughter, and it would have been over in a month or two. However, I decided to put my opinions aside and accept my daughter's opinion. I would let the young man call her and pursue a relationship with her.

This required a conversation with my daughter. I was going against my better judgment, and if I was going to support her, it required setting up expectations with the young man, expectations with his parents, and expectations with my wife. As things progressed, the young man was required to stay in communication with all involved. This relationship required a conversation about developing new boundaries as time went on and as things became more serious. It required conversations when I thought agreements were not being kept and reconstituting the agreements already made. After a year, they decided to call it off, and they both experienced the pain of ending something beautiful.

This is a pain my daughter will probably remember for the rest of her life (you still remember your first romance, right?), and I could have prevented this pain by holding on to my opinions. However, I strongly believe the lessons she learned and the experience she had watching me set aside my opinions while staying in full communication with her and not judging her helped her grow in her relationship with Christ. Of course, I am not saying we should always lay aside our opinions as parents, only that we need to consider our children's opinions.

STORY 15:
A Daughter Sacrifices Her Desires

Two years later that same daughter was about to graduate from high school and was preparing for her first year of college. While she was uncertain about what degree to pursue, she had decided on getting a paralegal certification. Right before graduation, she asked to have a talk with me, and off to my bathroom office we went. She was nervous and giggling, and she started with, "I have something to tell you."

To relax the moment, I asked if she was pregnant; she laughed and said, "No…but there is this young man who is interested in me, and I think he is really cool, so I would like to start seeing him." Given the availability of modern technology, I asked for his Facebook name so I could "stalk" him. He seemed like a good guy: he was Christian, he was going to school, he had served at the same camp as my daughter, and so on. However, my gut told me that my daughter needed to focus on her classes, not a man, at this time. Ultimately, I told her that she was old enough to make her own decisions; however, I was not for it and I told her why. To Tracey's and my amazement, she decided to lay down her opinion and accept mine, and she told the young man it was not the right time for her. Looking back, however, my wife and I should not have been amazed; my daughter's experience with the previous young man had taught her to trust me. In other words, giving up my beliefs then allowed her to trust me later.

A year later, she had one year left to get her certification, and she came to me and said, "I do not want to be a paralegal anymore. I have done the classes, earned straight As, and completed an internship with a lawyer, but I know I want to be a camp director."

With a heavy sigh, I said, "OK. I can go with 'camp director' if that is the dream God has put in your heart, but I strongly recommend you complete the paralegal certification as you investigate what it takes to be a camp director." She did not like that idea, but again, she laid down her opinions and accepted mine, taking the time to complete her paralegal certification.

Fast-forward another nine months, and she had completed the paralegal certification with a 3.8 GPA. She immediately applied for and received an assistant camp director job (is that amazing or what?). For her, the icing on the cake was that the young man she had not seen for over a year also returned to camp. She approached me again; this time I gave my blessing for them to start their courtship, and they did. This book will be published before we know how that ends, but we know it has a solid foundation.

In exchange for laying down her life, my daughter received a degree she could choose to use in the future, and her thinking, organizing, and analytical skills grew exponentially from studying law. She attained her dream job while knowing she honored the authority that God had in her life, and she even received the bonus of courtship with a young man she liked after they'd both matured. It's possible that none of this would have happened if I had not given up my beliefs regarding the first young man.

SOMETHING TO CONSIDER

What part of your life are you being called to lay down for your family?

7

Suppression or Expression: Which One Are We Cultivating?

Principle: Expression allows for correction and direction.

At ages two, three, four, five, six, and maybe even seven, eight, and nine, all of my kids were happy and lighthearted. Certainly they whined and cried occasionally, but they were spirited, joyful kids almost all the time. Then, between the ages of ten and eighteen, that joy became less frequent, and I found them to be self-reflective and serious, experiencing depression and other emotions rather than continual joy. What happened?

We could take the easy way out and blame it on their hormones. However, Christ did not say, "I came to give you life and more abundant life, *except* when your hormones are changing." Nor did Paul say, "We should exhibit the fruit of the Spirit, *unless* you're going through some change in life."

Therefore, consider that the lack of joy could be related to something else. I think it is related to many things, one of which is lack of expression. Parents unconsciously suppress their kids throughout their childhood and then wonder why their children do not talk to them. We wonder why they do not walk around smiling and laughing as they used to; we can't understand why they look depressed, angry, distant, or withdrawn. One reason I would have us consider is that most of our words and actions tell our kids what they cannot do or what they should do. Rarely do we tap into the dreams God has put into their hearts. Therefore, their immediate view of their future is clouded with the word "don't," and they do not have a clear view of where their hearts are leading them. When we can no longer see the dreams in our hearts, it is difficult to hold on to the spiritual joy that is available to us. When children are young, some of the dreams parents suppress are small and not noble in any way, but those dreams are the ones in the children's hearts. It is at this young age that we can encourage them to follow the dreams that God has put in their hearts. Let's look at one little example.

STORY 16:
She Just Wants to Talk to Her Dad

My second youngest girl had just turned seven when I wrote this page. If you asked people which of my children was the most cheerfully energetic child, they would undoubtedly point to this daughter. She constantly smiled and giggled. She didn't walk through the house; she cartwheeled from room to room. She was an extreme child in the area of joy.

One night, Tracey and I were talking about how I'd recently disciplined our daughter for something, and how I'd gotten irritated when she did not seem repentant. Tracey was quick to point out that this child basically had one emotional response: smiles and giggles. At seven years old, she was just plain happy.

Being seven, my daughter had recently discovered two things: the phone (any phone) and my cell phone number. For two full weeks, I received at least two, and sometimes five, calls a day on my cell phone. Luckily I have a job where I can answer my phone without disturbing others, so I answered the calls. At first, I loved these conversations. They usually went like this:

Daughter: Hi, Dad. What are you doing?
Don: Working.

Daughter: When are you coming home? Can you come home now?
(She said this in an excited, high-pitched, little-girl voice filled with the joyful anticipation of her father's homecoming.)
Don: I am not coming for three hours.
Daughter: Aw, Dad.
Don: Sorry, sweetheart. I will not be home until six-thirty.
(Then her chipper little voice would return. She would tell me she loved me, and that was it.)

The first few times this happened, it was cute. After a while, I started getting irritated. She would call and get my irritated "Do not call me; I am busy" voice. I even went to the extent of telling Tracey that our daughter should not be calling and that I needed her to control the kids.

Then it dawned on me: Did I really not want her to call me? I had caller ID, so if I really did not have forty-five seconds for this conversation, I could just refuse the call. However, if I did have forty-five seconds, why shouldn't I take the call and let her joyfully express her enthusiasm for our relationship? Fortunately, I caught on to this quickly, and I made up my mind to match her cheerful voice with my own cheerful voice. If you remember from chapter 6, our job is to lay down our lives for our children. For me, handling a forty-five-second phone call four or five times a day became no big deal because it was the desire of my daughter's heart!

This is a simple story about a simple desire. I am sure as you reflect upon your family, you can come up with your own stories. Look for the expression on your children's faces. When you see their love for you on their faces, then you watch it quickly drain out as you lecture them, you know you have entered the realm of suppression, and that path will lead to depression.

On the other hand, for our children to be expressive, especially as they get older, they have to know it is safe to say what is on their mind, even if they are absolutely certain we will disagree. The only way I know for us to impact our children's beliefs, especially in the areas where they disagree with us, is for us to know where they disagree. If it is not safe to disagree, children will not express themselves. They will not feel safe to speak if they are disciplined, lectured, or given dirty looks when they disagree. It will be safe for them to disagree if you ask them questions such as "That is an interesting thought; how did you come up with that?" or "Really, I did not think about it that way; did you think this up on your own, or did you read about it somewhere?" Anything that creates a dialogue with your child will encourage expression.

STORY 17:
A Discussion about the Future

When my son was eighteen years old, I was very intentional when discussing his future with him. When I asked about his future desires, he was hesitant, but he finally said that he was thinking about getting an engineering degree or possibly going into the ministry. My curious reply was "Are you serious about going into the ministry?"

He nodded his head. "Yeah, it is a serious consideration."

I said, "What about being a youth minister?"

He looked at me with a sheepish grin. Now, I know what the grin is about. For his whole life, I have told him that I totally disagree with the whole concept of youth ministers. I told my kids that I believe our youth should be taught by older women or men, not by young people coming out of seminary. Because of this belief, I limited my children's activities in the church youth ministry. The sheepish grin was really him saying, "Dad, if I tell you that I might want to be a youth minister, and we both know you disagree with that as a ministry, what are you going to say?"

Taking my own advice, rather than filling the moment of silence with "dad chatter," I kept my mouth shut, and I waited for him to speak. He finally said, "Dad, I know how you feel about youth ministers, but I do not agree with you. It is possible that I might want to do that." Happily, that day I was in the Spirit, not the flesh. I was able to respond that we would work together during his senior year to further develop his relationship with God. If the desire of his heart was still to be a youth minister, we would trust that God put that desire in his heart. This allowed him to express himself, and it also allowed us to have a continual dialogue where he could speak what was in his heart. If God guides the hearts of kings, I knew He could guide my son's heart, and I chose to trust the Lord to guide his heart.

Hopefully, you can see and hear that laying down my life for my son was actually laying down my opinions. More times than not, our insistence that our opinions are right or that our kids' or spouse's opinions are wrong stops all "real" communication. Instead of having dialogues with those closest to us, we end up lecturing one another, or at best, we have two separate conversations happening simultaneously. For a moment, and as you read the rest of this book, ask yourself, "What do my opinions cost me?"

SOMETHING TO CONSIDER

How can you listen to encourage expression?

8

Are Your Communication Style and Methods Producing the Children You Want?

Principle: Purposefully designing your communication method for each circumstance gives you an opportunity to produce your desired result.

Many books are written about communication between husband and wife and between parents and children. We have books on how miscommunications occur because we don't know how to listen to each other or because men think differently than women. A simple Amazon search for the topic "communications" comes up with over ten thousand books from which to choose. What could I possibly say in one chapter to impact your communication? Maybe it is that you can choose which communication style and methods you want every day.

First, we'll look at our Lord's communication style as outlined in both the New and Old Testament. We will look at the communication styles of the Father, Son, and Holy Ghost so that we get a very broad perspective; then I will give you good and bad examples from my family.

To prod your thinking, I've listed communication methods and styles from the Old and New Testament:

- God walked in the garden with Adam and Eve and, because he was looking for them, came to them in a non-omnipresent way (Genesis 3:8).
- He talked to Abraham, almost directly in his heart (Genesis 12:1–9).
- He told us that the earth and sky that we see every day communicate His existence (Genesis 1:6–8).
- He made animals, including donkeys, speak directly to his prophets (Numbers 22:30).
- He sent prophets including Jonah (Jonah 1:1–2) and John the Baptist (Mark 1:2–4) to speak to us for him.
- He spoke with actions as he destroyed Sodom (Genesis 19:24).
- He spoke through provision by providing bread and quail to the Israelites (Exodus 16:13–16) and by providing a pillar of fire and cloud to follow (Exodus 14:19–20).
- He walked on earth and lived, supped, and slept with His disciples (any of the four Gospels).
- He provided lengthy lectures on hillsides to multitudes of people (Matthew 5:1–12).
- He held private inquiries with a select few of the disciples to answer their questions (Matthew 11).
- He talked in parables that left some people clear and others confused (Luke 8:10).
- He made outrageous requests of people, such as asking the rich man to sell all his belongings and give to the poor (Mark 10:17–22) and asking Moses to lead His people out of Egypt (Exodus 3:10–22).
- He sent his people to carry his message and gave them instructions on what to take (Luke 9:3).

- He changed his instructions to suit circumstances when sending people out (Luke 9:3).
- He spoke to people in dreams (Genesis 46:2).
- He spoke to people in visions (Psalm 89:19).
- He spoke to people in various circumstances at their request (Judges 6:36–38).
- He speaks to people in writing through His written word.
- He combined miracles with exhortation, and He spoke forgiveness of people with advocacy (John 8:11).
- He was patient: He waited forty years while the Israelites walked in the desert (Numbers 14); He waited five thousand years before he sent His Son (see chronology in Matthew 1).
- He spoke through blessings (2 Chronicles 7:17).
- He spoke through curses (2 Samuel).
- He listened to appeals: He heard Abraham's appeal to the Lord (Genesis 18:22–33).
- He created clear, detailed standards (all of Leviticus).
- He promised to speak mercifully if we communicate (I John 1:9).
- He had His people communicate through song (Psalm 96).
- He communicated through example by having His Son live with us (Leviticus 26:12).
- He was aloof to the point that looking upon His face would cause our deaths.
- He created and revealed mysteries (Ephesians 3:2–6).
- He summarized difficult concept with simple statements.
- He communicated things about the future that we cannot possibly understand (Matthew 5:12).
- He made specific requests of us (Ephesians 4:32 and Exodus 20:12).
- He held the hearts of kings to guide our laws (Proverbs 21:1).
- He got angry with us (Numbers 32:13 and Psalm 30:4).

- He was loving, compassionate, and forgiving with us (Psalm 116:5).
- He spoke in a small voice in our hearts (Revelation 3:19).
- He communicated in a loud voice from the sky (Revelation 14:7).
- He wrote on walls (Daniel 5:5).
- He spoke with plagues (2 Chronicles 6:28).
- He spoke in foreign tongues (Isaiah 28:11-12).

As you read the list above, you should have started to see that God speaks to us in unlimited ways and takes advantage of every possible communication vehicle to help us understand that He loves us. He does not give up after telling us once or even twenty times; He organizes the whole world around us so that we get the message that He loves us. He finds a hundred ways to communicate what works and what doesn't in this life. He knows in advance that we are going to fail, and he finds a way to communicate that He will provide for us regardless. By examining how God communicates with us, we can see that we have many resources to communicate with our children and spouses. In fact, we can see how to communicate to our grandchildren before they are born. When we start looking from that timeless perspective, we can see that how we communicate to our children will provide new ways for them to communicate to their children. Our reach is well beyond our life when we look from God's timeless perspective.

Now this is an interesting conversation at best when looking at it theoretically. Let me present a couple of examples of creative communication that I have used with my family to jump start your thinking.

STORY 18:
Outwaiting a Son: Determined Patience

One Saturday morning, I was having a discussion with one of my sons, who was quite angry with Tracey and me. The way he expressed his anger was inappropriate and quite disturbing to the whole family system. When

I could not affect it with casual conversation in the living room, I asked him to go to his room so I could talk with him privately. We went into his room, and in my customary style, I sat on the floor while he lay on his bed. I started the conversation with words of "determination." I said, "Son, we are going to determine what the matter is and get it sorted out, and I am not leaving this room until we do."

This was a dangerous statement to make. Like most of you, I make plans—some mundane and some exciting—for my Saturdays, and this Saturday was no different. However, when I made this statement, I really thought that the resolution would take ten minutes at most. So I proceeded to ask questions about what was wrong, and he grunted, "Nothing," or remained altogether silent. We kept fairly close eye contact (in others words, I did not let him go to sleep). The more he said, "Nothing," the more I tried to guess why he was mad at Tracey and me.

After about thirty minutes of my guesses and his silence, I said something like, "Well, I have taken my best guess about what is wrong, and it is not acceptable for you to treat Tracey and I like this. Until you either let us know what is wrong or at least figure out how to articulate part of why you are upset, we cannot go forward." After another several minutes of silence, I added, "Well, I will simply sit here and look at you until you can figure it out."

At this point, I had been sitting there for nearly an hour, and I was getting antsy. On one hand, I did not want either of us to lose our Saturday sitting in his room. On the other hand, I did not want a weekend of tension in the house. After a few moments, I decided to stick to my original statement and keep my word. I had told him that I would continue sitting there until we figured it out and that I had nothing else to say. So I continued sitting there quietly.

I sat in that room for *four hours* with our young man. Finally, we did figure it out; the problem had nothing to do with Tracey and me, but we were feeling the brunt of his anger. Of course, it was something I never would have guessed. What's most interesting is that it wasn't until we had sat there for four hours that he realized that he *himself* did not know the root of his anger. It took that amount of reflection for him to discover the root, and we pulled it out together. (You're probably dying to know the issue, but that knowledge stays between him and me, and it is not related to this point.) The critical component of the conversation was my willingness to sit with him—not upset, not mad, not lecturing, just being with him—until he could sort it out for himself. I also think it was helpful that I was the person saying, "This will get worked out." As the father, I had the faith for him that he could sort it out.

This is one communication tool you must have: *determined patience.*

STORY 19:
Do Not Forget the Simple and Obvious

The best part about reading scripture with your children is not the everyday studying that one could do but the practical application that can occur. One afternoon I was sitting at the kitchen table with another of my sons, and we were discussing a dilemma in his life. He opened the Bible to what we were going to read that day, and it was exactly on point to his circumstance. I firmly believe he knew that in that moment, the God of the universe spoke to his heart. The opportunity for this to happen would have been missed if we did not read together, and it would not have happened if I had given a lecture about scripture rather than letting him say what he saw.

STORY 20:
Inviting Someone Else to Help Communicate to My Son

One of the lessons Tracey and I try to teach our children is how to work with and for others and how to have others work for God. My son Robert is an excellent carpenter, plumber, and general worker. However, I had not provided him the opportunity to be responsible for encouraging others who were working with him. To handle this next area of development, I put a bug in our youth minister's ear: I mentioned that on an upcoming mission trip to Mexico to build homes, it would be great if Robert could be the foreman on one of the houses. The youth minister,

Mike, graciously accepted my request, and my son received the news that he would have to manage his peers on this construction project. Now, Mike is as devious as I am, and he made me foreman of the other house we were building. The competition began to see who could motivate his team to finish its house first.

By enrolling Mike in helping me develop my son, I was able to expand Robert's experience. Now he had to look out for people's safety and health (it was August and extremely hot). He had to learn how to motivate kids who resented him being in charge, how best to use kids who wanted to do more, how to use kids who wanted to do more but could not hit a nail with a hammer if their salvation depended on it, and how to manage the boy-girl dynamic in a construction crew.

Robert and I reviewed his performance afterward. He told me it was very difficult for him to have his peers report to him, but that he'd learned that he could do it. He even fired two of the kids on his crew, demanding that I take them and trade him two of my kids. (I allowed it; I thought it was a very creative solution to handling his team members' rebellion.)

Mike was more than willing to help me develop Robert by giving him this life experience. If I had not been looking for different ways to communicate in my son's life, he would have been on a crew reporting to an adult, and he still would have had a lot of fun; however, he would not have learned these new skills if I hadn't enlisted Mike's help.

By the way, he won our competition, but only because on the third day…Oh, never mind. You don't want to hear my excuses.

Of course my son wasn't born with the ability to build a house and supervise other kids. He was trained over the years through Tracey's and my commitment to give him a wide scope of experience. The next story is about one of those times during the farming years.

STORY 21:

Communication through Challenging Projects

One of the experiences during the farming years that prepared my son Robert for the mission trip was a small construction project.

When we had the farm, Jimmy (not his real name) lived on the property with us and helped us with the farm. He had the combination of being extremely strong and yet being gentle with our kids. He had a powerful build; when I walked by the little house where Jimmy lived and he stepped out on the porch without his shirt, I would think, "Boy, I wish *I* was built like that!" In addition, Jimmy was extremely loyal. I could always trust that he wouldn't do anything to harm me, my family, or my little farming business. He came from the old school of thinking that you give a good day's labor for a good day's wage. The man worked like an ox for me, and given his gentle nature with the kids, both Tracey and I saw it as a blessing to have him on our property.

One drawback was that Jimmy had virtually no farming experience, and he was not necessarily great at building things on his own. He was wonderful to work with, but I would not feel comfortable leaving him alone with a major project. The other little quirk about Jimmy's old-school way of thinking was that he believed children should be submissive and quiet around adults. For instance, he would have considered it insulting if I left one of my children in charge of a project and he had to take direction from that child. This unique combination of strengths and weaknesses set the stage for one of the lessons I wanted to teach my son.

One fall day, I needed a greenhouse built and skinned (stretching the plastics over the PVC pipes). We needed to protect some plants because there was going to be frost that night. However, I needed to do some delivering and sales that day, and I could not be there to skin the greenhouse.

My son was twelve at the time. I knew that he knew how to skin a greenhouse, and he knew what mistakes not to make. However, at twelve, he did not have the strength to actually *do* all the work. His nine-year-old brother was a fabulous worker, but he didn't have the strength either. Meanwhile, Jimmy had never built a greenhouse before, and I knew that without my management, he would make enough mistakes that the greenhouse would not get completed in time.

In considering the problem, I saw the opportunity before me. I pulled my son aside and told him that it was important that the greenhouse get completed before nightfall, but I could not be there. Then I explained the dilemma. I told him that he was bright enough to know *how* to build the greenhouse but not strong enough. I added that Jimmy was strong enough but did not have enough experience. I also explained that Jimmy would resent taking direction from him because of his youth. I ended with this assignment: finish this greenhouse. I would put Jimmy in charge, but my son could not let Jimmy make a mistake, and he could not tell Jimmy what to do.

I said, "You are going to have to figure out how to honor Jimmy in a way that he will listen to you without being insulted."

With a twelve-year-old's grimace, he said, "Daaad!"

I said, "You can handle it."

Reluctantly, he said, "Yes, sir," and I left to deliver the radishes and cucumbers we had harvested that morning.

When I returned that afternoon, naturally I was eager to see what happened, but I was more eager to hear what my son had learned than whether or not they actually finished the greenhouse. To my delight, I walked back to the field to find Jimmy and my son standing next to each other with their eyes gleaming—the greenhouse was done. I walked up to them, shook both their hands, and said, "Thanks for getting it done; it looks perfect." (And it was.)

As we walked back to the house, I asked Jimmy how it had gone and whether my son was a good helper. Jimmy said, "It went great, and Robert did a fine job of helping me." I looked over at my son, and he smiled and winked at me. I knew then that I had taught my son how to empower others through service and humility. While my son knew and understood more, the project could not have been finished unless he served and provided his knowledge to Jimmy in a humble manner. No book or Bible verse could have taught Robert this lesson any better than this one day of working with Jimmy.

Today, think of the lessons you can create for your children that will effectively communicate the principles you want them to have.

SOMETHING TO CONSIDER

What are at least six different ways you can communicate to the people you love?

9

How Do We Encourage Our Children to Follow the Desires of Their Hearts?

Principle: When our children are committed to following Christ, He puts His desires in their hearts.

If you're willing to consider that God has put His desires for children in their hearts, then your job should be obvious. As paretns, we must help them discover those God-given desires and help them be responsible and accountable to pursue them. If you take this approach, you will run into a number of difficulties that you should be prepared to face head on:

- Their God-given desires may not be your desires for your children. What should you do about that? *Get over yourself.*
- They have not developed their self-reflection muscle, they are afraid to speak, and they might not know or might suppress their desires. What should you do about it? *Be patient.*

- Their desires may involve formidable challenges and look unreasonable. What should you do about it? *Help them overcome the obstacles.*

STORY 22:
A Championship Game

My youngest son has played sports since he was two years old, and because his older brother played basketball, this boy grew to love that game in particular. At twelve, we put him in a homeschool basketball organization; however, we decided (for a number of reasons) not to put him in the most competitive organization, mainly because it would take too much time away from the family.

Because becoming a great basketball player was his strongest desire, I decided to coach basketball, despite never having played the game in any formal manner. I started as an assistant, and when he turned thirteen, I became the head coach for his team.

Through many discussions, it became clear that he wanted to be on the best team and play basketball in college. However, there were a couple of small roadblocks:

- At thirteen, my son stood five feet five inches tall and weighed about ninety pounds.
- I knew nothing about basketball.
- Our organization was not competitive, and no one in leadership wanted to change that.

To tackle these problems, my son worked extra hours to be great and to understand the game. I read books and watched videos for hours, and I decided to transform the organization into a competitive one. Finally, I declared to the organization that we would become one of the eight best homeschool teams in the nation with a 6A ranking.

When my son reached high-school age, he had greatly improved his game and had enrolled a number of friends who were very inexperienced players to work as hard as he was working. I enrolled the organization to allow more practice time and to allow us to play tougher teams, even though we lost many games. At one point, we had lost twenty-two games in a row.

The year before my son made the varsity team, that team placed sixty-fifth (out of seventy-two teams) in our national tournament. It was not looking good for him to obtain the desire of his heart.

During his junior year in high school, I became the head varsity coach. Despite all the circumstances, I continued to trust that God put the desire in my son's heart to make 6A and to play college ball. Based on this belief, I continued to work with the kids and to tell them we were going to make it, despite the fact that some of my own players laughed when I prayed before nationals, "Lord, it is our desire to get to 6A." Some parents even complained that I was setting the kids up for failure. That year we failed and ended up in 2A (far below our target).

In his senior year, my son and I continued to believe and work to make 6A. Many of his friends had improved dramatically, and the team spirit and energy were wonderful. That year, I announced to the team that our spiritual emphasis during devotions would be Philippians 4:6-7:

Do not be anxious about anything, but in everything, by prayer and petition, with thanksgiving, present your requests to God. And the peace of God, which transcends all understanding, will guard your hearts and your minds in Jesus Christ.

Before each game, no matter how tough a team we were playing, I prayed, "Lord, I want you to know that it is the desire of our hearts to win this game. While I want the players to play hard and show the right attitude, have no mistake, Lord our desire is to win this game." At first, this did not go over well with the parents. It took them a while to realize I was training the players to be honest with God, and I was trusting that God would give them peace even if they lost because they had been honest about their desires. For me, it sure beat the prayer "Let the best team win"; that would not have been honest.

When we eventually won our first three games at nationals and made it to 6A, there was quite a celebration. We ranked eighth out of seventy-two teams at nationals. We even received a special blessing and won the next two games, and we played for the National Championship in front of seven thousand people.

One of my fondest memories before that game was when my assistant coach came to the championship game in a brand-new shirt with our organization's logo on it. I asked, "How'd you get that new shirt?"

He replied, "I bought this shirt at the beginning of the year and have been saving it for this championship game."

He believed in the dream. We lost that championship game, but years later, when I see my former players, I ask them what they remember most about that year. They never hesitate to say, "Pursue your dreams, and let God know your desires; peace will follow."

Finally, my son did get to play college basketball. In fact, six of my former players played college basketball, two with full scholarships, one of whom was the young lady I mentioned in chapter 4.

STORY 23:
A Young Man Discovers a Passion

At the age of twenty, one of my sons had still not really discovered a desire that he thought God had put in his heart. We could only stay in the inquiry and give him opportunities to try different things to see if anything stirred in his heart. Then one year, he had an opportunity to go alone to help a friend of ours, a missionary in Romania. He went to build a house for a family who had been living in a cardboard shack. He ran into numerous obstacles with this project, the main one being that the land the family had chosen was seized by the government, and he was running out of time. However, with only five or six days left on the mission trip, someone donated a house structure without windows or a roof, and my son was able to get to work and build the house.

My very task-oriented son was on a tight time frame and working diligently when one more roadblock was put before him: the missionary group he was with insisted on praying for two or three hours right in the middle of the workday. After a while, my son embraced the concept and trusted that this was necessary to get the job done—and eventually, the job got done. As a result, on this trip, he discovered his passion for prayer and mission work. He became an engineer, and he is now married. He continues to lead prayer groups in our church, and he sponsors and plans mission work to the Dominican Republic every other year.

I tell you this story to demonstrate that that remaining patient and providing opportunities can help your children stay in the inquiry about what desires of their heart are God-given. Inquiry combined with patience creates opportunity for discovery.

SOMETHING TO CONSIDER

Do your children know the desires of their heart that God put there? If so, how can you foster them? If not, how can you help your child discover them?

Conclusion

I have shared with you principles to dwell on and things to consider in how to raise your family. Some of them sound easy, some sound difficult, and you may be lost on how to implement them. The good news is that implementing life principles is a lifelong process, not an exercise you do once. You will learn from your own mistakes and victories. Every day provides opportunities to learn a little more about yourself and your Creator.

You might ask, "With which principle should I start". Of course my answer is a question. What is your current state of mind? If you are angry, depressed or upset (not who you say you are) you might start with asking yourself questions like:

- What does my reaction reveal about my heart?
- What am I wrong about?

If you are operating in the spirit and need to help someone else you might ask yourself:

- How can I express love now?
- How can I listen to encourage expression?
- How can I respond creatively here?
- Is there a different way to communicate this principle?

The above questions are examples, consider spending some time generating your own questions to ask yourself. By having these questions ready, you have taken the first step in renewing your mind. As your mind is being renewed and you spend time meditating with God, you will be able to trust that when life happens and one of these questions jumps to the front of your mind, it is the right question to ask yourself, because the Holy Spirit has prompted you.

Your decision to use the principles in this book is not as important to me as you embracing the idea that your path to raising your children is the key to you becoming more like Christ. You will do great because Christ is within you.

May God bless your family, and may you be open to His grace and hear His voice.

Note to my children, grandchildren, great grandchildren and so forth:

My youngest daughter, Cheryl, was helping me complete the final proof of the book, and she said, "Dad, the conclusion is short, which is nice; people will not have to read too much, but you might want to end the book with a final story." We brainstormed for a few minutes, and I decided that rather than telling a final story, I want to request that my children start a new family tradition.

The current family tradition is when our children reach the age of 13 we invite them to read the book Preparing for Adolescence by James Dobson. After they complete the book, we go somewhere fun and exciting for the day and discussed the book between activities. The point of the discussion is to invite them to create their own standards for their relationships with their parents, friends, and future spouses.

The field trips changed over the years depending on my children's interests. Two sons experienced deep-sea fishing. My oldest daughter enjoyed a private fishing trip; my next daughter decided that a day of shopping would be fun, and finally, Cheryl chose a day of horseback riding. (I got to rustle some cattle, fulfilling one thing on the bucket list.)

My request to my children is: When your kids are 13, ask them to read this book. Then schedule an exciting, fun-filled day with them to discuss their impression of the book. Use the time as a catalyst for them to discover their own dreams for the future. Invite them to consider embracing the principles presented in the book or to develop some of their own. Tell them Grandma and Grandpa love them, and we are looking down smiling. I write these final words with tears in my eyes.

Author's website: www.DesignedtoLove.org

Made in the USA
Middletown, DE
18 February 2022

61503701R00056